Backyard Books

Are you a Butterfly?

For Anna M.– J. A.

For Beth, Daz, and Tom
and especially for Clair—T. H.

KINGFISHER
a Houghton Mifflin Company imprint
222 Berkeley Street
Boston, Massachusetts 02116
www.houghtonmifflinbooks.com

First published in hardcover in 2000
First published in paperback in 2003

6 8 10 9 7 5

(HC) 5TR/0603/TWP/DIG/1508EM

LIBRARY OF CONGRESS CATALOGING-IN-PUBLICATION DATA
Allen, Judy.
Are you a butterfly? / by Judy Allen; illustrated by Tudor Humphries.—1st ed.
p. cm.–(Backyard books)
Summary: Introduces the life cycle of a butterfly, showing how it changes from an egg
to a chrysalis to a butterfly.
1. Butterflies—Juvenile literature. [1. Butterflies.] I. Humphries, Tudor, ill. II. Title.
III. Backyard books (New York, N.Y.)

QL544.2 .A445 2000   99-045777

Editor: Katie Puckett
Coordinating Editor: Laura Marshall
Series Designer: Jane Tassie

Additional research: Warren Collum

Printed in Singapore

ISBN 0-7534-5240-5 (HC)
ISBN 0-7534-5608-7 (PB)

Are you a Butterfly?

Judy Allen and Tudor Humphries

KINGFISHER
BOSTON

Are you a butterfly?

If you are, your parents
look like this.

You start your life
in an egg like this.

As soon as you are strong
enough, break out of it.
You do not look like your
mother or father.

You are
a caterpillar.

You have
sixteen legs, a
hairy back with
tiny breathing holes in it,
and very small eyes. You have no
nose, but you do have
a mouth.

So eat.

Eat whatever you are standing on.

Your mother laid your egg on
a delicious leaf.

Grip the leaf with your legs to hold
it steady. Then eat it.

Now eat the next leaf.

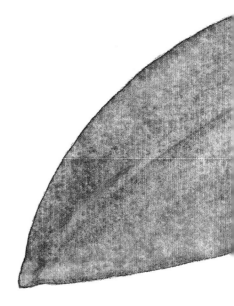

Eat every leaf you can reach.
Then move to another bunch of leaves
and eat them, too.

You grow **bigger**.

And **bigger**.

Eat more.

You feel full.

You feel so full you think
you are going to burst.

You are right,

you ARE going to burst.

Before you burst,
glue yourself onto
a leaf or a stem so you
won't fall off.

Your skin will split
all the way down
your back.

Don't panic.
This is normal.
Climb out of your old skin.

You may have to wriggle
around a bit
to do this.

As you eat and grow,
you will have to climb
out of your skin two
or three more times.

One day you will feel funny.
It is time to find somewhere safe
and glue yourself to it.

You are going to make a chrysalis.

You may not be able to spell it,
but you will be able
to do it.

You will change while you are in your chrysalis. You will change a lot.

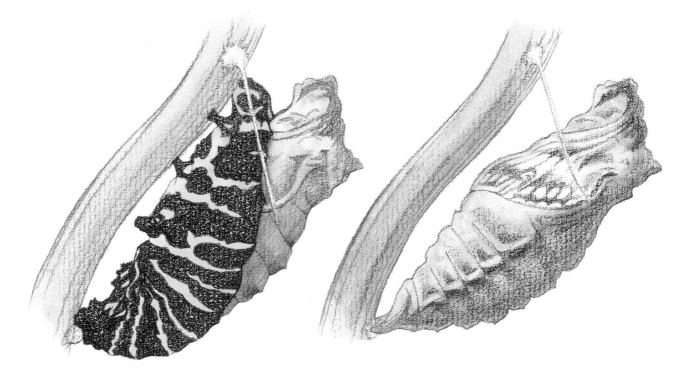

You will grow six legs instead of sixteen. You will grow large eyes instead of small eyes.

You will grow long feelers on your head.
You will grow wings!

When you have done
all of these things,
break out of your
chrysalis.

Your wings are crumpled.
They look terrible.

Don't worry. Hang upside down
from your chrysalis.

Slowly, slowly,
your wings will stretch.
The creases will all go away.

Use the long feelers on your head to smell flowers.

Use your long tongue to drink nectar from the hearts of the flowers.

Use your wings to fly!

However, if you look
a little like this

or this

or this, you are not a butterfly.

You are not even a
caterpillar.

You are . . .

. . . a human child.

You have no wings.

You can't fly.

It is most unlikely that you have
long feelers growing out of the top
of your head.

But you can do a lot of things that butterflies can't do.

You will never have to make a chrysalis.

And you will never,

ever, EVER

have to eat so much your skin splits.

Did You Know . . .

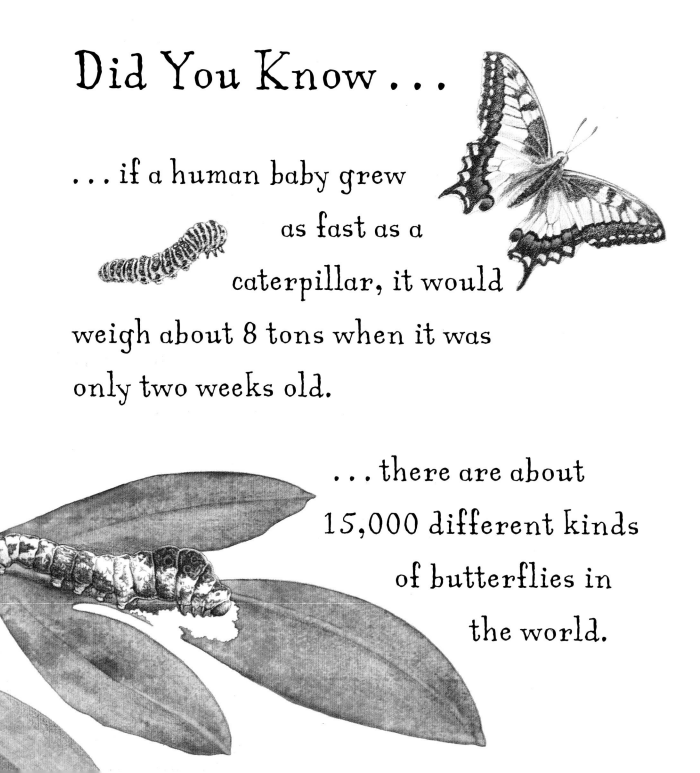

. . . if a human baby grew
as fast as a
caterpillar, it would
weigh about 8 tons when it was
only two weeks old.

. . . there are about
15,000 different kinds
of butterflies in
the world.

. . . the Queen Alexandra butterfly of Papua New Guinea is the largest in the world—when its wings are spread out, it measures 11 inches across.

. . . butterfly wings are covered with thousands of tiny, brightly colored scales. Never touch a butterfly's wings. They are easily damaged, and if the butterfly can't fly anymore, it will die.